Women of the Black Panther Party

Credits

This book was created by
The West Oakland Mural Project
home of
The Women of The Black Panther Party Mural
in West Oakland, California.

The Mural and this book are dedicated to brilliant and brave
Women of The Black Panther Party.
Thank you for everything.
Love, The World

Special thank you to Ericka C. Huggins and M. Gayle 'Asali' Dickson,
whose support and guidance on this project has been immeasurable.

Copyright © 2020 by Jilchristina Vest

All rights reserved. No part of this publication may be reproduced, distributed, or transmitted in any form or by any means, including photocopying, recording, or other electronic or mechanical methods, without the prior written permission of the publisher, except in the case of brief quotations embodied in critical reviews and certain other noncommercial uses permitted by copyright law. For permission requests, write to the publisher, addressed "Attention: Permissions Coordinator," at the address below.

Producer and content	Jilchristina Vest
Lead Advisor	Ericka C. Huggins
Lead Historian	Angela D. LeBlanc-Ernest
Graphic Design	Creative Shields -James Shields & Krista Kang Turner
Images and Drawings based on	Stephen Shames Photography
Muralist	Rachel Wolfe Goldsmith

Printed by
Community Printers 777 W Grand Avenue, Oakland, CA, 94612

Second Edition 2021

www.comprinters.com
www.westoaklandmuralproject.org
www.erickahuggins.com
www.creativeshields.com
www.rachelwolfegoldsmith.com
www.angelaleblancernest.com
www.stephenshames.com

Hello Children, big and small!
Welcome to the Women of the Black Panther Party Activity Book.

It is our pleasure to introduce you to this activity book both as co-contributors to the #SayHerName Women of The Black Panther Party Mural as well as collaborators united in our passion for education, children and preserving the history of The Black Panther Party and its Survival Programs.

Members of the Black Panther Party (BPP) were young, ambitious, and filled with love for all people, committed to change locally and internationally. The fight for human rights was the goal. The members of the BPP fought for that right from the 1960s to the 1980s. When Huey P. Newton and Bobby Seale imagined and created the organization in Oakland, California, on October 17, 1966, they started a movement that lit imaginations and changed the lives of thousands of future members and supporters of freedom around the world. They sat together in Oakland and wrote the Black Panther Party 10-Point Platform and Program. It was a call for basic human rights. Point 10 of the Platform is a summary of them all: "We want land, bread, housing, education, clothing, justice and peace."

Women of the Black Panther Party quickly became a main foundation for improving human lives in the U.S. Like many freedom movements throughout history, women were the backbone of the BPP. Tarika Lewis, a sixteen-year-old high school student, asked to join and became the first woman member of the BPP. Many young Black women like Tarika, an artist and violinist, filled the roles of boots on the ground community organizers, Central Committee leaders, Survival Program administrators, BPP Newspaper writers, artists and editors, community board members, teachers, mothers and grandmothers. They were coalition-builders who learned from the people on the job.

Women of the Black Panther Party were harassed and attacked by federal and local law enforcement in the same way as the men of the BPP. Whether they worked in the Bay Area, Philadelphia, Boston, New Orleans, Atlanta, Winston-Salem, Houston, or abroad in Algeria or Tanzania, they sacrificed their lives to challenge the old ways that served a few, to work toward implementing the Ten Point Program, to serve many.

Of course, the BPP made mistakes along the way, as young organizers with an average age of 19, they tried to fashion a new world that blended ways of thinking and created solutions to worldwide problems using the teachings from a variety of international revolutionary women and men of that time. These thinkers and doers helped party members to face the reality that most men and some women, were raised or trained to believe that boys and men are smarter and stronger than women and girls.

Just as millions are taught that the lives of people of color, black, brown and indigenous (Native) people are less valuable than the lives of white people. As well, the ideas that it's best to be rich in money and that if you live in conditions of poverty, it's your fault. Indeed, women of the BPP challenged themselves and the men to rise to a higher standard, to dig deep inside themselves, and do the work required to rebuild Black and other poor communities. At the center of their struggles, was a love for humanity; a big heart for the people. This activity book honors the lives of Women of the Black Panther Party, seen and unseen, alive and in the ancestral realm, who dedicated their lives to uplifting the quality of life for Black and poor communities. This book is a companion to the West Oakland Mural Project and the #SayHerName Women of The Black Panther Party mural dedicated to women of the BPP. We know that one mural and one little book will never do full justice to the beauty of these women's lives.

However, it is a starting point for learning more. These pages contain a concentration of information about some of the women in the Black Panther Party; the most information that has ever been amassed.

Yet, we hope that this small tribute will spark greater interest. May it function as a springboard for more research and the collection of more oral histories and materials that archive the lives of women of the BPP. More importantly, we hope that this activity book will inspire young women

and men today to make a positive difference in their communities, wherever they live in the world.

Black Panther Party members, women and men alike, did not wait for the right time. They declared that the time for change was/is now. All Power to all the People!

With Love,
Angela D. LeBlanc-Ernest
and Ericka C. Huggins

www.angelaleblancernest.com
www.erickahuggins.com

Ericka C. Huggins

Angela D. LeBlanc-Ernest

Connect the Dots

Complete the official pin for The Black Panther Party.

Be creative! Show your individual style!

BLACK PANTHER PARTY

PANTHER POWER

The Black Panther logo was born in the SNCC (Student Non-Violent Coordinating Committee) movement, initially representing the Lowndes County Freedom Organization in Alabama. Artist and SNCC member Ruth Howard was the first to sketch it.

Discover where The Black Panther Party was founded.

Unscramble the Word

LADAONK

___ ___ ___ ___ ___ ___ ___

1966 Newton and Seale founded The Black Panther Party (BPP) while they were students at Merritt College and as a result helped create the first Black Studies classes.

RANK and FILE

By 1969 the majority of their members in The Black Panthers were women. By the mid 1970's, at the height of The Black Panther Party membership, women made up 70% of The Black Panther Party.

Using the list below match The Black Panther Party's community survival programs with the picture.

Match + Color

| Sickle Cell Anemia Research Program | Free Dental Program | Child Development Center | Food Co-Op Program | George Jackson Medical Clinic | Free Legal Aid and Education Program |

Maze

Drive safely while you deliver free groceries to community members, but watch out for dirty cops.

START

FINISH

Celebrate your natural hair! Color by numbers to discover the message in The Black Panther's Afro.

Color by Numbers

Choose Your Colors: 1 2 3

Word Search

The Black Panther Party worked hard to create and manage more than 60 Community Survival Programs.

Can you find 16 of them in this word search?

```
P O I E U Y T R E W Q A S D F G H H
M B O D A U J D I A L A G E L H C Q
O R A U E R M H O U E G Z X Y R L A
K E D C V N O D N T R R W T A S O Z
N A B A H I T C A F D O A E W C T X
B K E T A N H I G L O C S R N I H S
H F L I I A A N S G H E L M U N I W
U A D O E T I B R T R R A I V I N E
G S A N X T C A N L S I J N B L G D
Y T E F O E S M L O K E F A E C L C
V S H V B R L E N E G S R T T E P V
C C H I L D C A R E G Y W O A E O B
A G U M S E V C A N W Z O R H R M F
F O O D L W E E I E S P N S D F J E
J U I K L O I S V G Y S R O T C O D
S H C H U B U C R E V T R G O N U A
L I I O N O P A M B U L A N C E N L
S K Q E H R R E V U L X T I N Y H L
```

WORD BANK

- Ambulance
- Breakfast
- Clothing
- Childcare
- Dentists
- Doctors
- Education
- Exterminators
- Food
- Free Clinics
- Groceries
- Housing
- Legal Aid
- Lunch
- Sickle Cell Research
- Voting

THE BLACK PANTHER
INTERCOMMUNAL NEWS SERVICE 25 cents

THE BLACK PANTHER PARTY

The first issue of The Black Panther Newspaper was published on April 25, 1967. It grew to a full newspaper and ran until September 16, 1980. During this time editors of the paper included Joan Kelley, Elaine Brown, Ericka Huggins and Judy Juanita.

M. GAYLE 'ASALI' DICKSON

In 1970, at the age of 22, M. Gayle 'Asali' Dickson joined the Seattle Chapter of The Black Panther Party.

She was a lead artist for The Black Panther Party Newspaper. Her graphics, centered around women and children graced the paper's back page.

Sister Asali was a pre-school teacher at The Oakland Community School and is the artist behind the school's logo.

The Black Panther Party registered thousands of people to vote across The United States. You have signed up to register people in your city.

Make a sign to help rally people to register and vote!

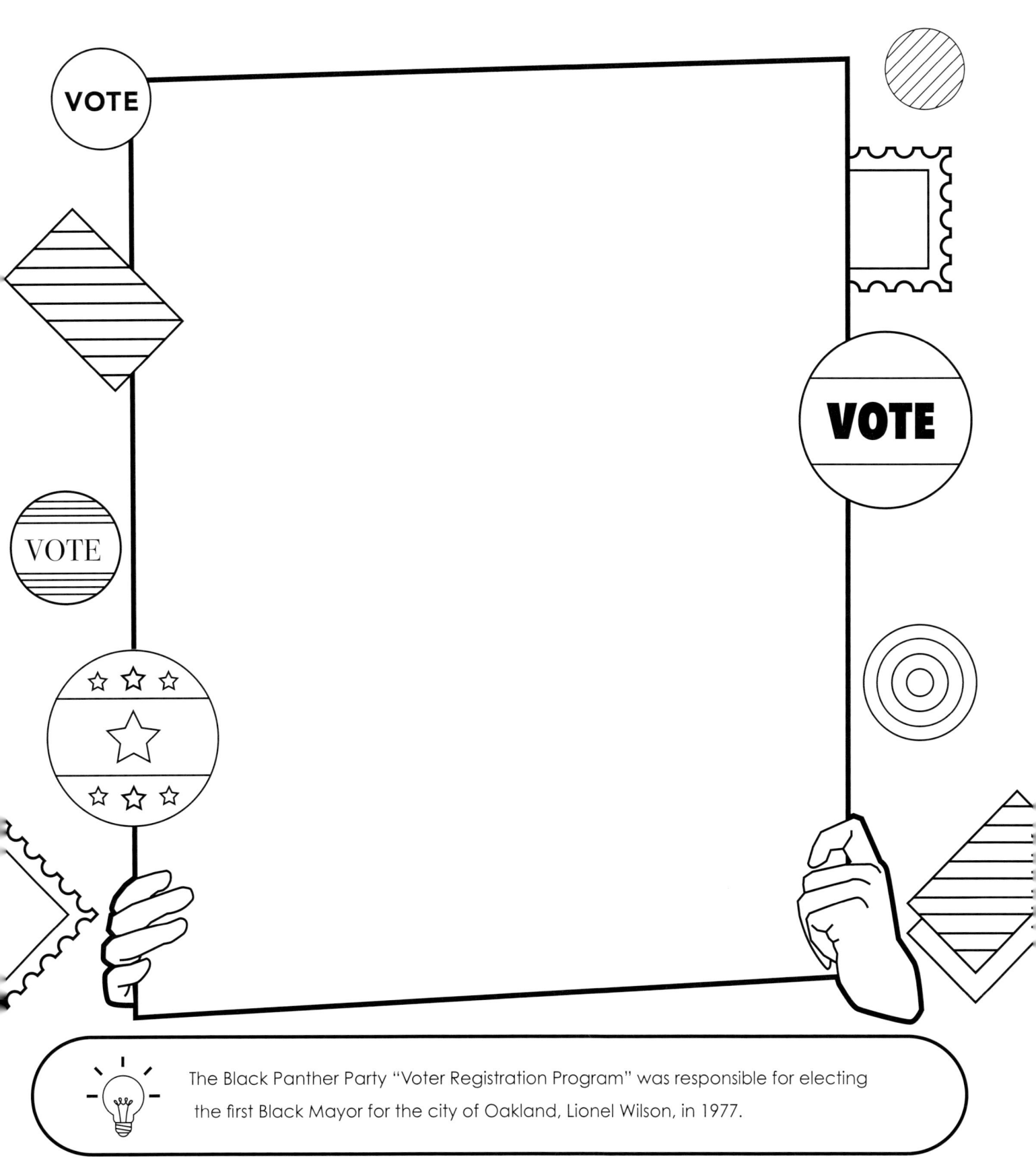

The Black Panther Party "Voter Registration Program" was responsible for electing the first Black Mayor for the city of Oakland, Lionel Wilson, in 1977.

This rank and file Panther is prepping bags of groceries for the Community Free Food Program. Spot the 10 differences.

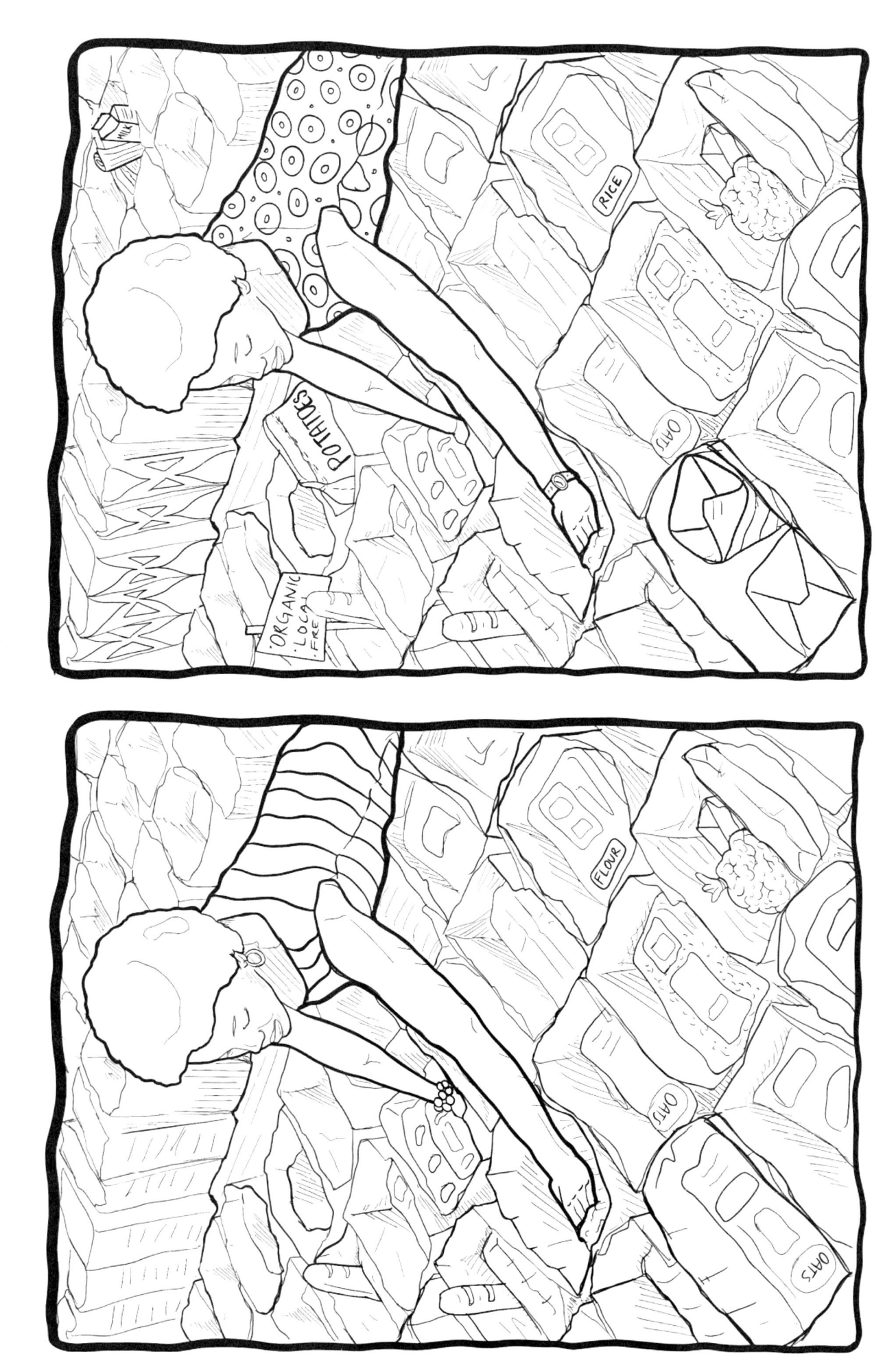

The Oakland Community School

"We teach children how to think not what to think". Encouraging students to think critically helps remove faulty thinking and non-factual conclusions.

Can you write about a time that you practiced how to think vs. what to think, to help you solve a problem, accomplish a goal, or learn something new?

Writing Activity

The Oakland Community School (OCS), established in 1973, in East Oakland was the longest standing Survival Program. Ericka Huggins and Donna Howell were the initial directors.

Good morning! It's 5am and hungry students are waiting in line for breakfast. Choose which ingredients you will serve for today's meal.

Initiated in January 1969, at St. Augustine's Church in Oakland, California, The Free Breakfast Program became so popular that by the end of the year, the Panthers set up kitchens in cities across the US, feeding over 10,000 children every day before they went to school.

The community center is your safe space where you and your friends play sports, make art, and are tutored.

Create an ad to help save your local neighborhood's community center.

Writing Activity

NEWS

SAVE OUR COMMUNITY CENTER

16

THE 10 POINT PROGRAM

1 WE WANT **FREEDOM**
We want power to determine the destiny of our Black Community, (and oppressed communities).

2 WE WANT **FULL EMPLOYMENT** for our people.

3 WE WANT an **END TO THE ROBBERY** by the white man (the capitalist) of our Black and oppressed) communities.

4 WE WANT **DECENT HOUSING** fit for shelter of human beings.

5 WE WANT **EDUCATION** for our people that exposes the true nature of this decadent American society. We want education that teaches us our true history and our role in the present-day society.

BPP Goals

6. WE WANT all Black men to be **EXEMPT FROM MILITARY SERVICE** (free healthcare for all Black and oppressed people).

7. WE WANT an immediate end to **POLICE BRUTALITY AND MURDER** of black people (other people of color, all oppressed people inside the United States.)

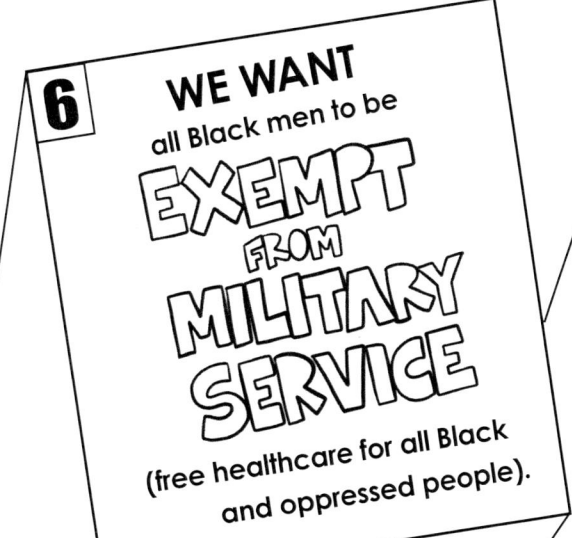

9. WE WANT (freedom) for all Black people (and poor oppressed people, held in U.S. federal, state, county, city and military prisons and jails.) **JURY OF THEIR PEER GROUP** We want trials by a jury of peers for all persons charged with so-called crimes under the laws of this country.

8. WE WANT FREEDOM for all Black men held in federal, state, county and city prisons and jail.

10. WE WANT LAND, BREAD, HOUSING, CLOTHING, JUSTICE, PEACE. And as our major political objective, a United Nations-supervised plebisciteto be held throughout the black colony in which only black colonial subjectswill be allowed to participate for the purpose of determining the will of black people as to their national destiny. (People's community control of modern technology.)

The 10-point program's was introduced to the public in 1967. In 1972, edits were made to reflect the plight of all disenfranchised groups of people throughout the world.
***(The 1972, revisions are highlighted in the noted copy marked by parentheses.)

JOAN TARIKA LEWIS

Born and raised in Oakland, California. Tarika became the first woman to join The Black Panther Party in 1967, at the age of 16.

Already an accomplished violinist she put her music career on hold to join the movement.

Tarika was a graphic artist as well and her art appeared in The Black Panther Party newspaper under her pen name 'Matilaba'.

She was an expert marksman as a Lieutenant in The Black Panther Party. Tarika was responsible for training new recruits.

Match the Panther to their contribution in the movement.

Crossword Puzzle

ACROSS

3. Was Communications Secretary and the first woman in the Party's decision-making body.
4. Escaped prison and lives in exile.
5. Ruth Howard, Dorothy Zellner and Lisa Lyons are the three women who drew and designed this logo.
6. Safiyah Bukari's book about being a Black Panther.
7. A member of The Black Panther Party and the Young Lords at the same time.
8. Kansas City chapter member and key member of The Black Panther Party's International contingent.

DOWN

1. Chaired The Black Panther Party from 1974 until 1977.
2. National Coordinator of The Free Breakfast Program.
9. Panther that played key roll in chapters from Oakland, Philadelphia, New York, and the international chapters.

WORD BANK

Barbara Easely-Cox / Charlotte O'Neal / Joan Kelley / Kathleen Cleaver / Elaine Brown / Assata Shakur / The War Before / The Panther Logo / Denise Oliver-Velez /

You and your friends are going to a "Free All Political Prisoners" rally.

What will your sign say?

LEGENDARY PANTHERS

KATHLEEN CLEAVER
San Francisco, California - Chapter Communications Secretary.

BARBARA EASLEY COX
Philadelphia, Pennsylvania - A key member of the International Chapter of The Black Panther Party.

CHARLOTTE O'NEAL
Kansas City, Missouri - Founded United African Alliance Community Center in Tanzania, Africa.

ASSATA SHAKUR
Oakland, California - She lead the community education programs, escaped prison and lives in exile.

Design a Book Cover

Panther members wrote books, essays, and speeches about their experiences and fight for a liberated society. Design the cover for your latest book.

What will it be about?

- ASSATA — Assata Shakur
- LOOK FOR ME IN THE WHIRLWIND
- MY LIFE W/ THE BLACK PANTHER PARTY | Akua Njeri
- AFENI SHAKUR — Jasmine Guy
- VIRGIN SOUL — Judy Juanita
- LIVING FOR THE CITY | Donna Murch
- INSIGHTS and POEMS — Ericka Huggins & Huey P. Newton
- SERVING THE PEOPLE: SURVIVAL PROGRAMS OF THE BLACK PANTHER PARTY / JoNina Abron-Ervin
- ONE CRAZY SUMMER — Rita Williams-Garcia
- A TASTE OF POWER — Elaine Brown
- THE WAR BEFORE — Safiyah Bukhari
- THE REVOLUTION HAS COME — Robyn C. Spencer
- ANGELA DAVIS

These books and hundreds more have been written by and about The Black Panther Party.

23

LEGENDARY PANTHERS

AFENI SHAKUR
Harlem, NY - Section leader of The Black Panther Party. Mentored and trained new members.

ELAINE BROWN
Oakland, California - Chaired/ Lead The Black Panther Party from 1974 until 1977.

ANGELA DAVIS
Los Angeles, California - Joined The Black Panther Party in 1967. Left in 1968 to join Communist Party, remained an ally.

JOAN KELLY
Los Angeles, California - National leader/organzier The Free Breakfast Program.

Maze

Find the path to freedom!

ALL POWER TO THE PEOPLE

START ▶ FINISH ▶

Identify all U.S. Black Panther Party Chapters:

Geography

Match the names of the states with the map to identify all Black Panther Party Chapters in the United States from 1966 to 1982.

MATCH THE STATE NAMES AND NUMBERS

1. _____
2. _____
3. _____
4. _____
5. _____
6. _____
7. _____
8. _____
9. _____
10. _____
11. _____
12. _____
13. _____
14. _____
15. _____
16. _____
17. _____
18. _____
19. _____
20. _____
21. _____
22. _____
23. _____
24. _____
25. _____
26. _____
27. _____
28. _____

WORD BANK

California / Colorado / Connecticut / District of Columbia / Georgia / Iowa / Illinois / Indiana / Kansas / Kentucky / Louisiana / Maryland / Massachusetts / Michigan / Missouri / North Carolina / Nebraska / New Jersey / Nevada / New York / Ohio / Oregon / Pennsylvania / Tennessee / Texas / Virginia / Washington / Wisconsin /

Geography

The Black Panther Women were instrumental in developing the international arm of the party.
Can you identify the countries where they had chapters, supporters, and allies

___ Algeria ___ China ___ North Korea ___ Japan ___ France ___ India ___ Palestine ___ Vietnam
___ United Kingdom ___ New Zealand ___ Denmark ___ Australia ___ Germany ___ Bermuda ___ Tanzania ___ Israel

MATCH THE COUNTRY NAMES

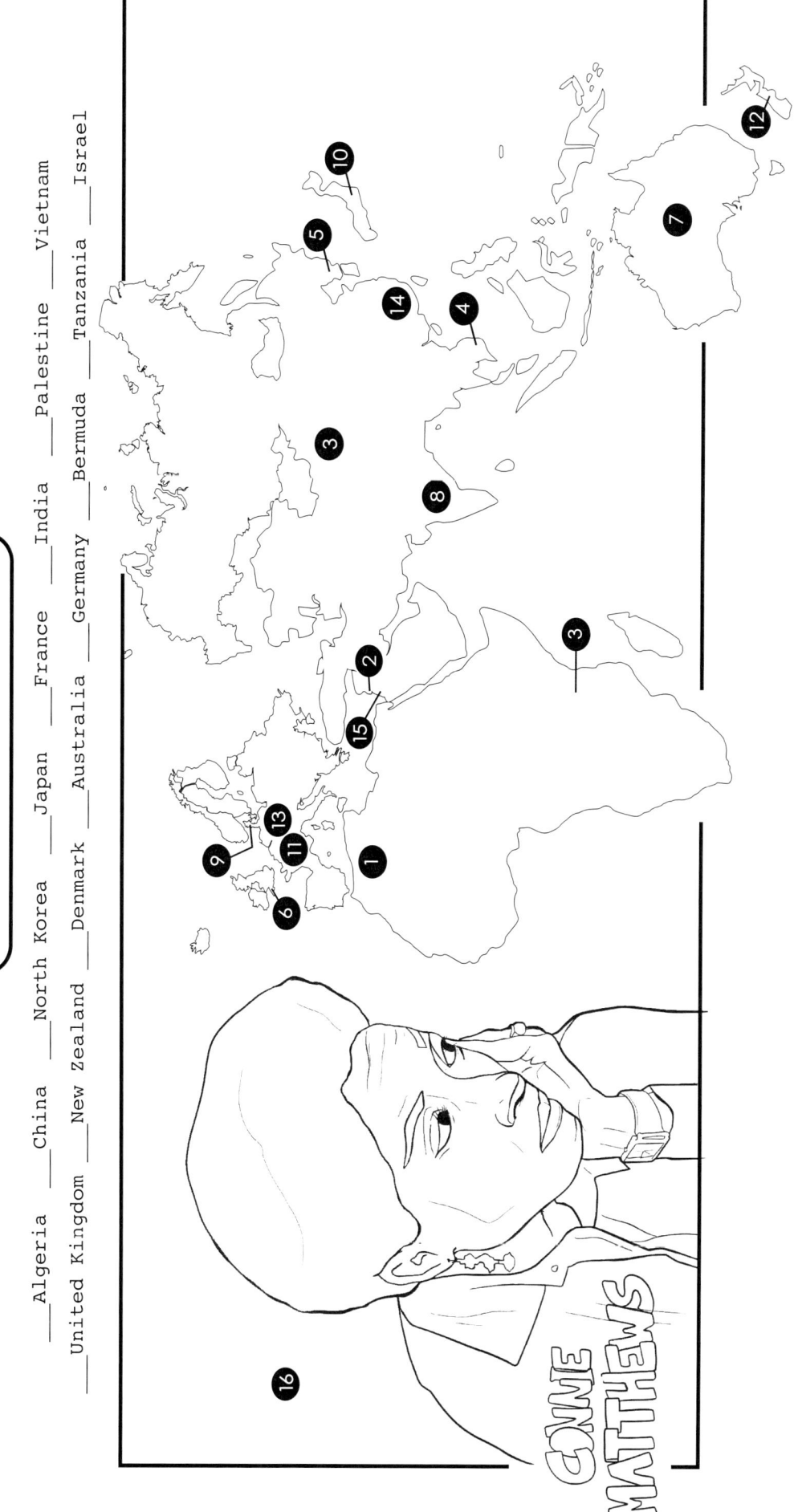

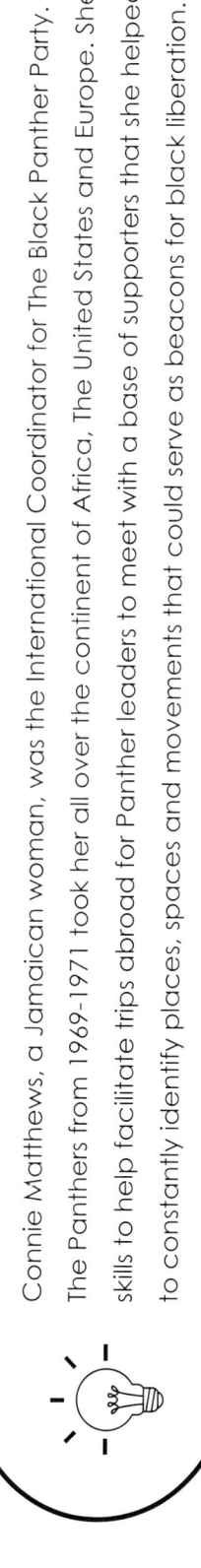

Connie Matthews, a Jamaican woman, was the International Coordinator for The Black Panther Party. Her work with The Panthers from 1969-1971 took her all over the continent of Africa, The United States and Europe. She used her contacts and skills to help facilitate trips abroad for Panther leaders to meet with a base of supporters that she helped cultivate. She was able to constantly identify places, spaces and movements that could serve as beacons for black liberation.

CONNIE MATTHEWS

THE SOLEDAD MOTHERS

Mrs. Inez Williams

Mrs. Doris Maxwell

Mrs. George Jackson

These brilliant and courageous women are the mothers of the Soledad Brothers (incarcerated Panthers) - Fleeta Drumgo, John Cluchette, and George Jackson. They are pillars in The Black Prison Movement.

Connect the Dots

Match the Panther to her contribution in the movement.

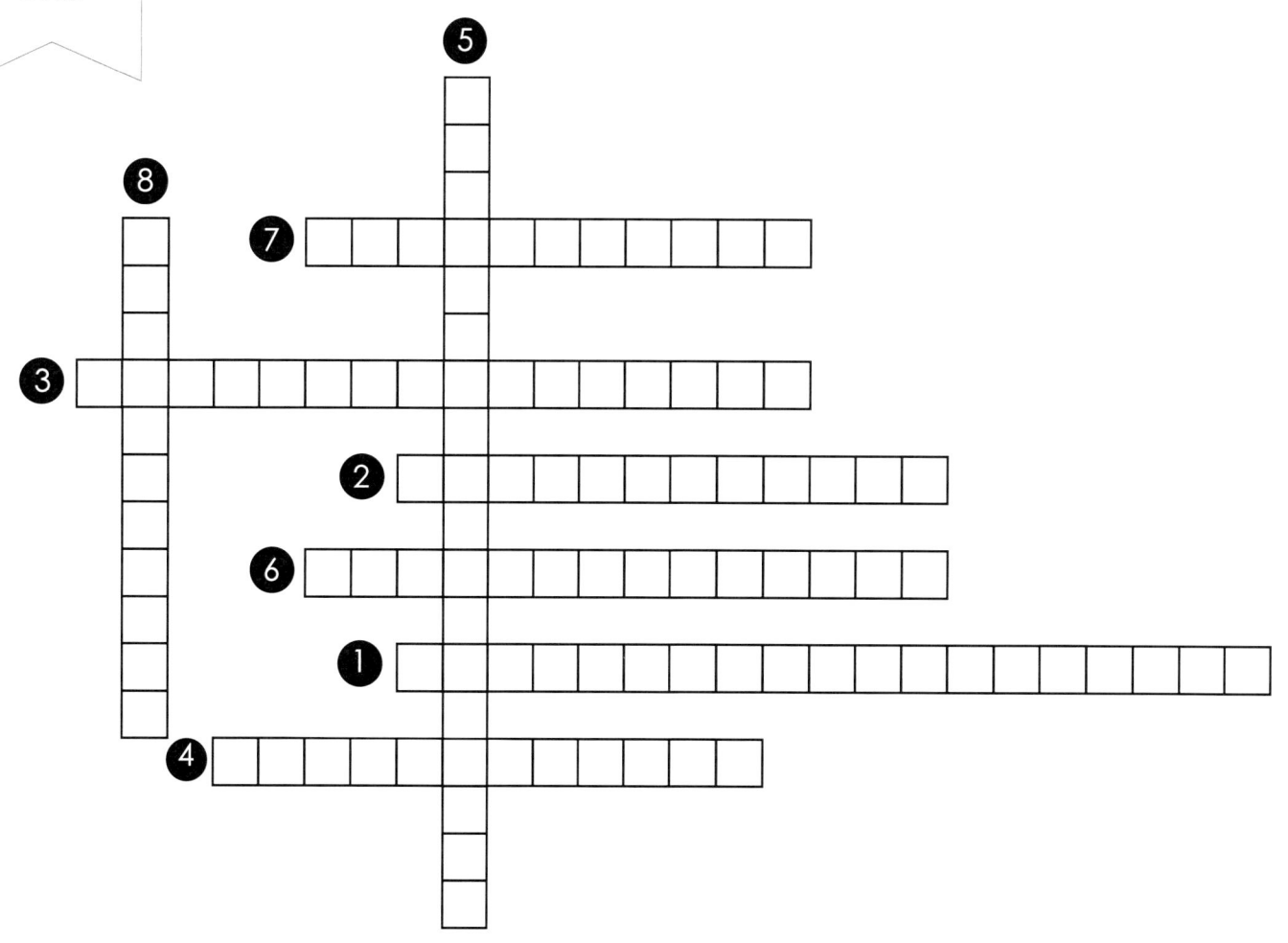

ACROSS

1. She wrote "One Crazy Summer".
2. Title of Elaine Brown's book.
3. Book written by Ericka Huggins and Huey P. Newton.
4. An accomplished violinist and the first woman to join The Black Panther Party.
6. Author of "Poetry" and "The Black Panther Party".
7. Author of "Virgin Soul".

DOWN

5. Panther who designed the Oakland Community School logo.
8. Wrote for The Black Panther Newspaper and mother of hip-hop icon Tupac.

WORD BANK

Taste of Power / Judy Juanita /
Insights and Poems / J. Tarika Lewis /
M. Gayle Asali Dickson / Regina Jennings /
Afeni Shakur / Rita Williams-Garcia /

The Black Panther Party launched over 60 Community Survival Programs based on the immediate need of the people. Can you identity the five pictured below?

Match + Color

| People's Co-Op Housing Program | Bus to Prison Program | Free Plumbing Program | Free Pest Control | Ambulance Program |

Thank you!

Create a Slogan to Energize The Black Panther Party!

INDEX

10 Point Program, 21-22

Afeni Shakur, 23, 24, 29

All Power to the People, 25

Ambulance Program, 37

Angela Davis, 23, 24

Assata Shakur, 18, 20, 23

Barbara Easley-Cox, 18, 20

Black is Beautiful, 8

The Black Panther, Newspaper, 10

The Black Prison Movement, 28

Bobby Seal, 3

Bus To Prison Program, 30

Charlotte O'neal, 20

Child Development Center, 6

Community Survival Program, 6, 9, 30

Connie Matthews, 27

Denise Oliver-Velez, 18

Elaine Brown, 10, 18, 24

Ericka Huggins, 10

Food CO-OP Program, 6

Free Breakfast Program, 15

Free Dental Program, 6

Free Legal Aid and Education Program, 6

Free Pest Control, 30

George Jackson Medical Clinic, 6

Huey P Newton, 4

Insights and Poems, Ericka Huggins and Huey P. Newton, 23, 29

Joan Kelley, 10, 18, 24

Joan Tarika Lewis, 17, 29

Judy Juanita, 10, 29

Kathleen Cleaver, 18, 20

Living for the City by Donna Merch, 23

Look for me in the Whirlwind, 23

Mayor Lionel Wilson, 12

Merritt College, 4

M. Gayle Asali Dickson, 11, 29

My life with the Black Panther Party, Akua Njeri, 23

One Crazy Summer by Rita Williams-Garcia, 23

Oakland Community School Logo, 11, 14

Panther Logo, 3, 18

People's CO-OP Housing Program, 30

Political Prisoners, 19

Rank and File, 5, 13

Rita Williams-Garcia, 29

Regina Jennings, 29

The Revolution Has Come by Robyn C. Spencer, 23

Ruth Howard, 3

Serving the People (Survival Programs of the Black Panther Party), JoNina Abron-Ervin, 23

Sickle Cell Anemia Research Program, 6

The Soledad Mothers (Mrs. Inez Williams, Mrs. Dorris Maxwell, Mrs. George Jackson), 28

SNCC (Student Non-Violent Coordinating Committee), 3

St. Augustine Church, 15

A Taste of Power by Elaine Brown, 23, 29

Virgin Soul by Judy Juanita, 23

Voter Registration Program, 12

The War Before by Safiyah Bukhari, 23

ANSWER KEY

P. 3

P. 4

P. 8

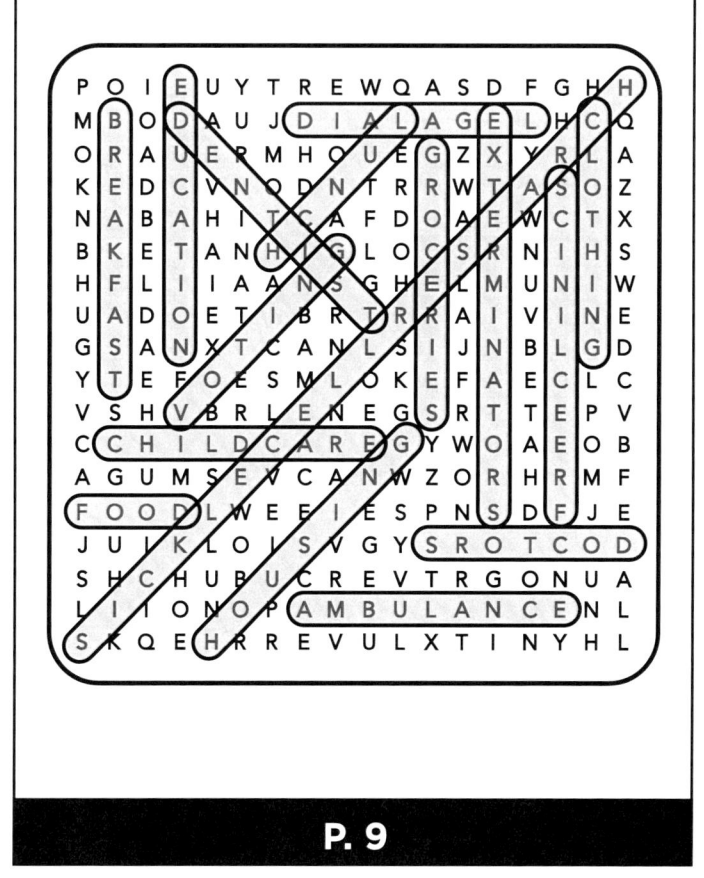

P. 9

ANSWER KEY

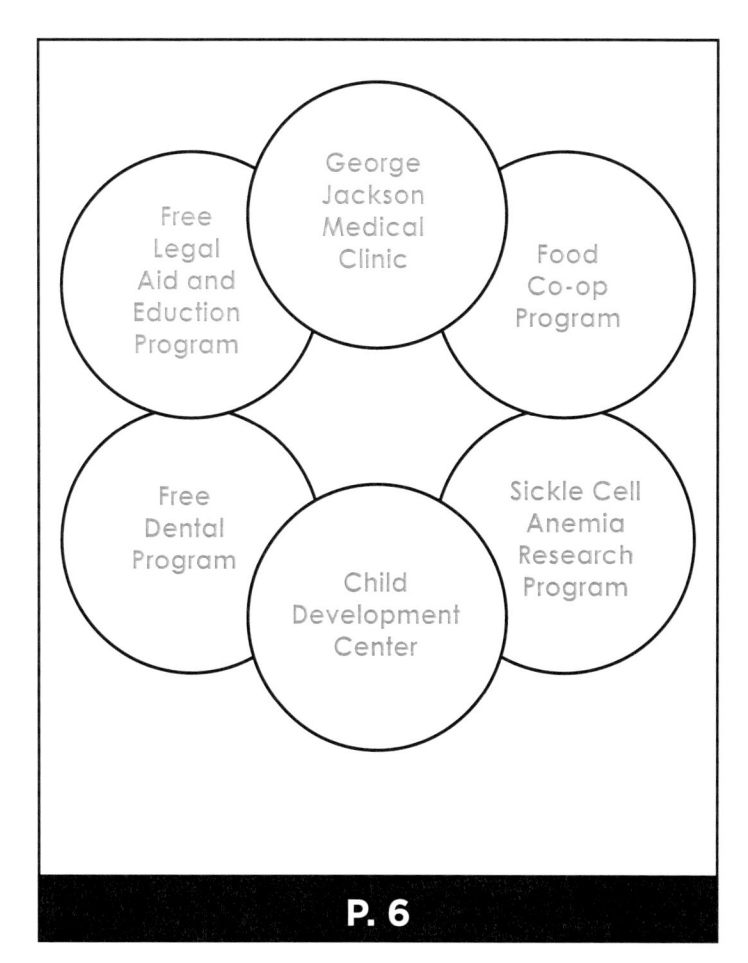

P. 6

- Free Legal Aid and Eduction Program
- George Jackson Medical Clinic
- Food Co-op Program
- Free Dental Program
- Child Development Center
- Sickle Cell Anemia Research Program

P. 7

P. 13

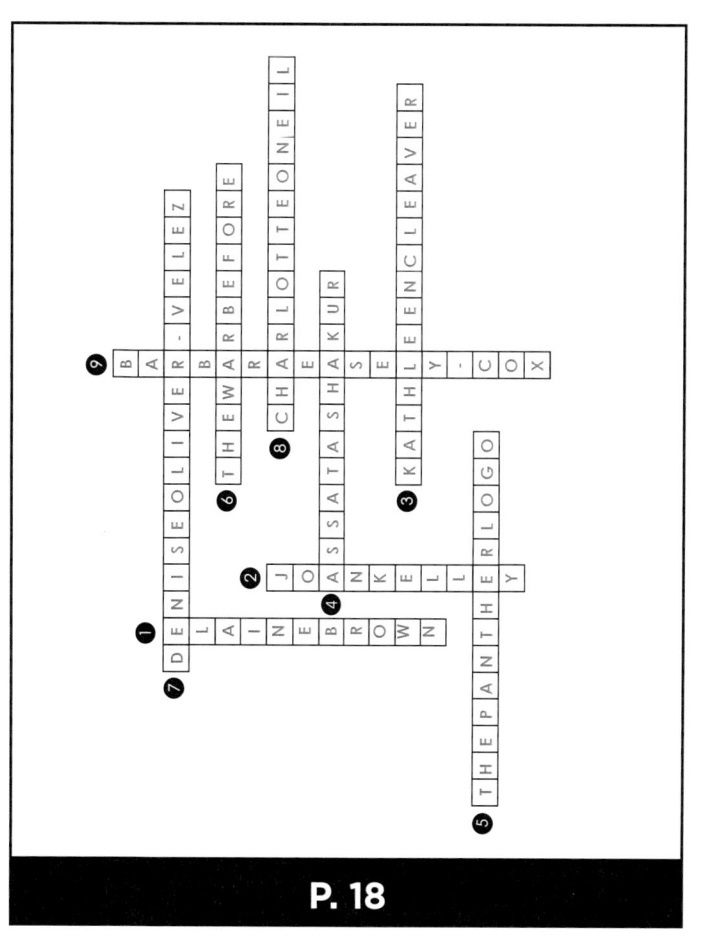

P. 18

1. DENISEOLIVER-VELEZ
2. JOANKELLY-COX
3. KATHLEENCLEAVER
4. ASSATASHAKUR
5. THEPANTHERLOGO
6. THEWARBEFORE
7. ELAINEBROWN
8. CHARLOTTEONEIL
9. BARBARA

Answer Key

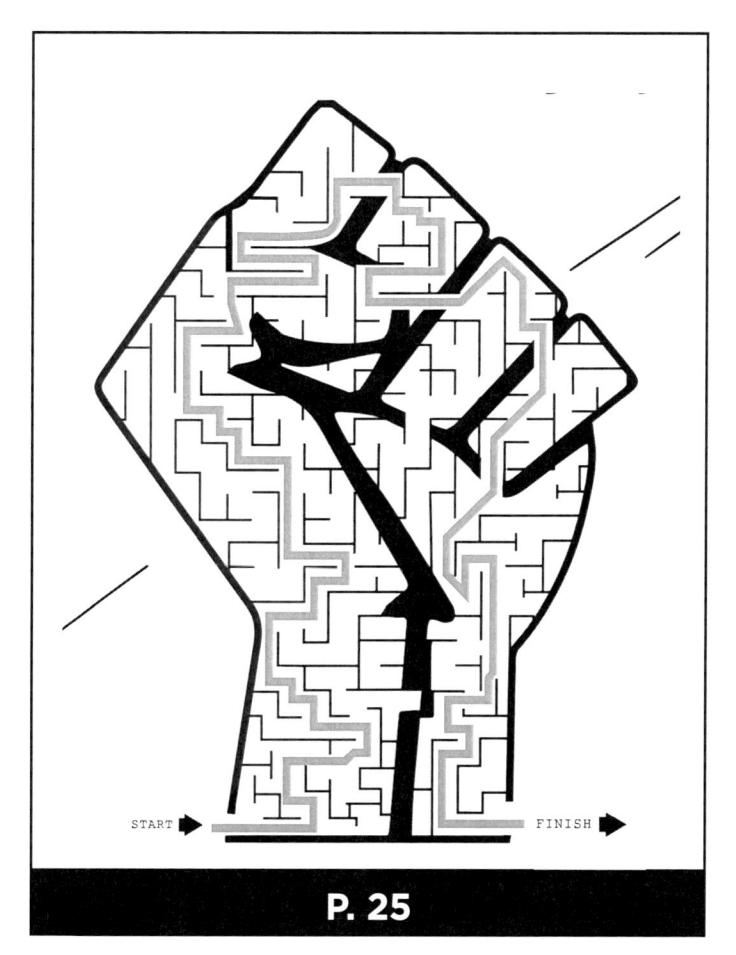

P. 25

P. 26

1	California	15	Texas
2	New York	16	Kentucky
3	Nebraska	17	Ohio
4	Georgia	18	Illinois
5	Louisiana	19	Nevada
6	Massachusetts	20	Connecticut
7	Virginia	21	District of Columbia
8	Missouri	22	Tennessee
9	Oregon	23	Wisconsin
10	Pennsylvania	24	Iowa
11	Colorado	25	Michigan
12	New Jersey	26	Washington
13	Maryland	27	North Carolina
14	Indiana	28	Kansas

P. 30

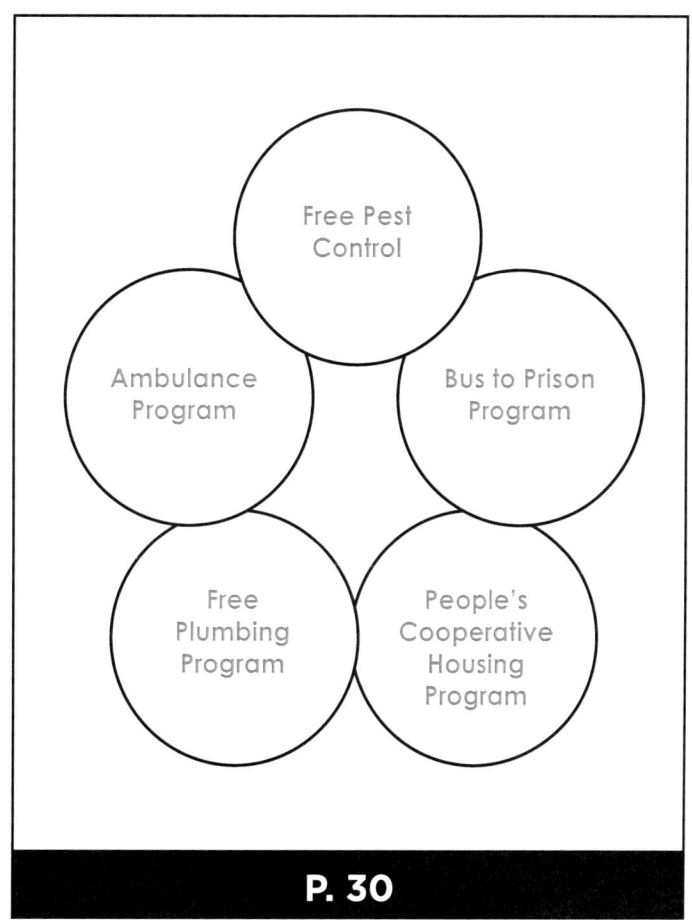

- Free Pest Control
- Ambulance Program
- Bus to Prison Program
- Free Plumbing Program
- People's Cooperative Housing Program

Answer Key

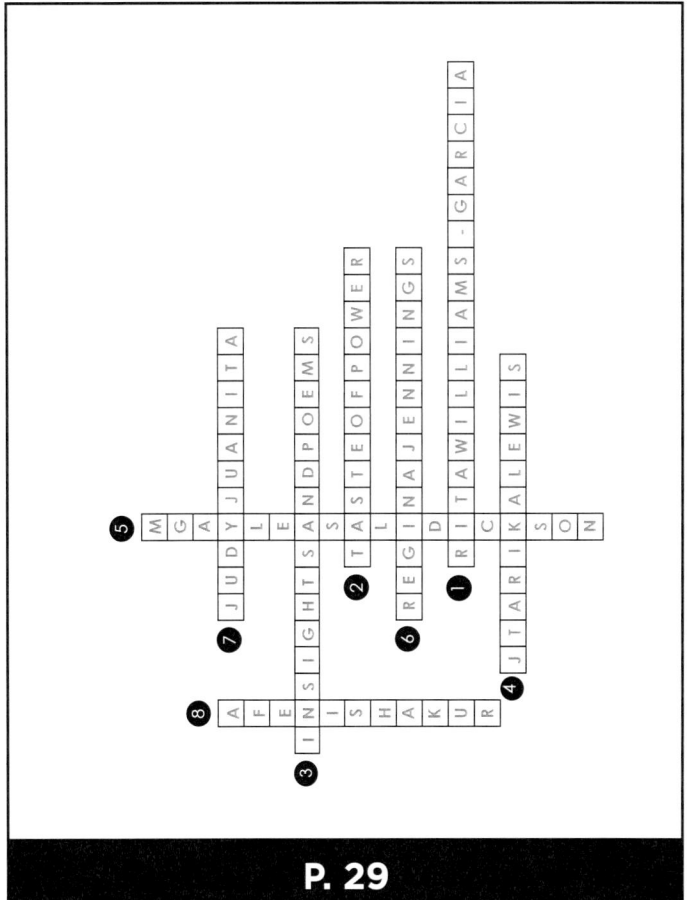

P. 27

1. Algeria
2. Palestine
3. Tanzania
4. Vietnam
5. North Korea
6. United Kingdom
7. Australia
8. India
9. Denmark
10. Japan
11. France
12. New Zealand
13. Germany
14. China
15. Israel
16. Bermuda

P. 29

1. RITA WILLIAMS-GARCIA
2. TASTE OF POWER
3. INSIGHTS AND POEMS
4. JTARIKA LEWIS
5. MGAYSON
6. REGINA JENNINGS
7. JUDY JUANITA
8. AFENI SHAKUR

support   Encouragement   Cooperation

For more information on the
#SayHerName
WOMEN OF THE BLACK PANTHER PARTY MURAL
please visit wbppmural.com